CEREDIGION
Interpreting an Ancient County

CEREDIGION

Interpreting an Ancient County

J. Geraint Jenkins

ISBN: 0-86381-961-3

Cover design: Sian Parri

First published in 2005 by
Gwasg Carreg Gwalch, 12 Iard yr Orsaf, Llanrwst, Wales LL26 0EH
☏ 01492 642031   🖷 01492 641502
🖱 books@carreg-gwalch.co.uk   Internet: www.carreg-gwalch.co.uk

CONTENTS

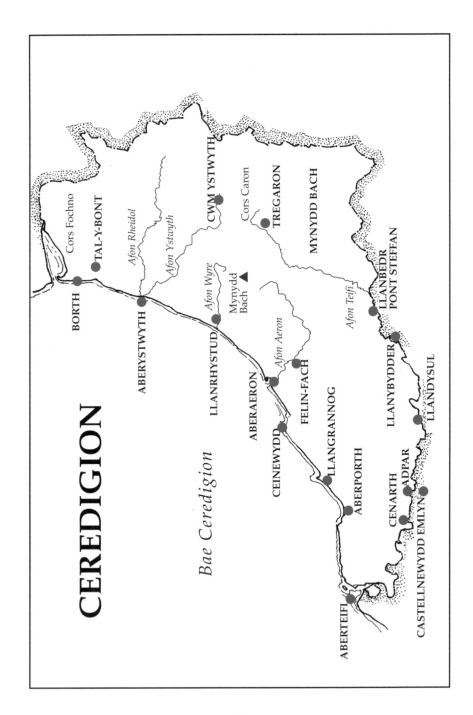

CEREDIGION

Bae Ceredigion

BORTH
TAL-Y-BONT
Cors Fochno
Afon Rheidol
Afon Ystwyth
ABERYSTWYTH
CWM YSTWYTH
Cors Caron
TREGARON
MYNYDD BACH
LLANBEDR PONT STEFFAN
Afon Wyre
Mynydd Bach
LLANRHYSTUD
Afon Aeron
ABERAERON
Afon Teifi
LLANYBYDDER
LLANDYSUL
FELIN-FACH
CEINEWYDD
LLANGRANNOG
ADPAR
LLANYBYDDER
ABERPORTH
CENARTH
CASTELLNEWYDD EMLYN
ABERTEIFI

PREFACE

Ceredigion is one of the few counties in Britain that has not changed its borders to any extent since the kingdom of Ceredig was founded soon after the departure of the Roman Conquerors from these islands. In the middle of the 5th century Cunedda, an important official under the Roman army brought an army from southern Scotland to dispel the large number of Irish settlers that had settled and caused a great deal of trouble in western Britain. Cunedda had eight sons and one of them – Ceredig was given a piece of land between Afon Dyfi (*afon* : river) in the north and Afon Teifi in the south and was crowned king of that kingdom.

The Land of Ceredig with its unique character and personality still exists as the county of Ceredigion. This volume explores some of those elements from the past that have contributed to that character. Over the centuries, Ceredigion has received much and has suffered much, but just like the jetsam left on the shore by the receding tide, Ceredigion has clung to its centuries of cultural development, despite many invaders, and the settlement of many alien people. For here in the fastness of Atlantic Europe there has been a continuation and a persistence of many aspects of life that can be traced back to the dawn of civilisation.

In the life of the people of this western corner of Wales at the beginning of the 21st century, elements from the distant past are still recognisable and no one can hope to understand or appreciate this land without looking at history and the influences from the past that has shaped its destiny.

Invaders from across the sea – Roman and Viking, Anglo-Saxon and Norman all came and left their mark on the land. Itinerant Celtic missionaries who brought Christianity to Britain, the industrial barons of the 19th century, the Anglicised aristocracy and even the tourists of the 20th century have all left their indelible footprint on the life and land of Ceredigion.

GLOSSARY OF WELSH PLACE-NAMES

Abergwaun	*Fighguard*
Abertawe	*Swansea*
Aberteifi	*Cardigan*
Bae Ceredigion	*Cardigan Bay*
Caerdydd	*Cardiff*
Caerfyrddin	*Carmarthen*
Castellnewydd Emlyn	*Newcastle Emlyn*
Ceinewydd	*New Quay*
Llanbedr Pont Steffan	*Lampeter*
Llandudoch	*St Dogmaels*
Ystrad Fflur	*Strata Florida*

ACKNOWLEDGEMENTS

With the exception of those acknowledged in the text most of the illustrations are from the collections of the Museum of Welsh Life of the National Museum and Galleries of Wales.

1
INTRODUCTION

The county of Ceredigion, stretching from the mouth of the Teifi in the south to the estuary of the Dyfi in the north, is an area of scenic and cultural variety. Its long coastline, with its ageless tradition of fishing and seafaring and its many small villages that seem to cling to the edge of the land differs very greatly from the isolated moorland sheep runs of the north east, beyond Tregaron and Llanddewi Brefi. The well-forested Teifiside with its splendid mansions of a disappeared aristocracy on the banks of a gently meandering river, differs very greatly from the flat monotony of Cors Fochno. The rivers that flow westwards into Bae Ceredigion – the Rheidol, Ystwyth, Wyre, Aeron and others provide fingers of green lushness contrasting sharply with the rounded, bare hills of the surrounding upland, where life was a constant battle against the gorse, heather and ferns that always threatened to take over the limited pockets of fertile land.

There are also difference between the inhabitants of the various parts of the county. The river Wyre, small though it is, is said to have been a linguistic boundary between the south and north and Dewi Sant himself would not venture beyond that northern boundary. The coastal dwellers of Ceredigion were outward looking; many of them travelled to all quarters of the globe and to the young men of those sea-locked villages there was no way of life other than going to sea. Many of the county's earliest settlers came to the region by sea and in later centuries the seas around south-western Wales became the well-travelled highways of Celtic missionaries who first brought Christianity to these islands. As time progressed, the communities that lived in the coastal areas of Ceredigion became more and more isolated and more cut off from the society of the land and of landward living, agricultural communities. The mariners and the landsmen becamae alienated.

The small coastal village of Llangrannog is typical of the sea-orientated settlements of Ceredigion. It is located at the mouth of a small rivulet, the Hawen, that flows through a gorge-like valley with sharply rising gorse and bracken clad hills which rise steeply on both flanks of the village, and cut down to a minimum the social contact between the village and the agricultural communities in its hinterland. Throughout the centuries, the inhabitants of this village had no outlook other than the Irish Sea and by tradition the sea played a vital part in its development. Like so many Ceredigion coastal villages, the settlement was founded by a Celtic missionary of the sixth century to whom the sea was a highway rather than a barrier. In later centuries there was constant travel across the Irish Sea. The local aristocracy found it much easier to send their offspring to be educated in Dublin rather than elsewhere. The needs of the fishing industry were imported from Ireland and many of the women of the village purchased Irish fabrics. As recently as 1900, almost all the male inhabitants of Llangrannog were associated with seafaring either as sailors, fishermen or merchants. Ships were the topic of every conversation; far away places were household names and the names of the large shipping companies were as well known to the inhabitants of the coastal villages of Ceredigion as were the names of the familiar Non-conformist ministers. The coast supported outward-looking communities and the villages developed their own special character and personality.

Life on the coastal rim contrasted very sharply with that of the central core of upland which is so dominant in Ceredigion. That area supported a population that was inward looking, and that went no further than the boundaries of its own immediate neighbourhood for the means of life. To the upland dwellers, life was almost a scavenging existence of gathering from the mountains, fields and bogs and processing the harvest within their own communities. Upland Ceredigion is an ancient and isolated land where the old and the new co-existed side by side until recent times. The technology born of Abraham Darby's blast furnaces in the Severn Gorge took longer to penetrate the fastness of Wales' central core than to cross the oceans to the Americas and Australasia. In a relatively poor community where the margin between survival and starvation was a very narrow one, a family had to depend on its own resources. To the hill farmer, life was a constant battle against the elements; heavy rainfall and bleak conditions could destroy the labour of years. The income of the hill farmer in the past was very low as he had few cash crops that he could sell on the open market. There were severe constraints on higher output; the prospects of arable farming were poor and upland pastures sterile. The hill farmer could never afford the elaborate and expensive implements of tillage that were demanded by the more fortunate lowland agriculturist. Neither could he go beyond a staple diet of home grown food for his family. To till his land and fence his fields, he was forced by circumstances to depend on his own ingenuity to make the best use of the resources available to him. This ingrained poverty may be the reason why the native of Ceredigion, the Cardi, has the reputation of being amongst the most careful and thrifty of all the inhabitants of the British Isles. Of course things may have now changed in upland Ceredigion and it may be far more prosperous than at any other time in its history but, undoubtedly the centuries of battling against a hostile environment has affected the character of the society.

Life was never as hard in the lush valleys of Ceredigion as it was in the uplands. Nature was kinder here, the soil was better and there was shelter for man and animal. Dwellings were far more comfortable and the valley villages supported numerous craftsmen who supplied the community's needs. In addition, a plentiful water supply provided power for a variety of small industries such as wood-turning and textile manufacturing which generated wealth for the workers. The village of Dre-fach Felindre for example, although a few miles outside the boundaries of Ceredigion, developed into an important industrial village during the second half of the nineteenth century. Because the inhabitants of the village relied entirely on industry, rather than agriculture, their outlook became more akin to that of the inhabitants of the industrial valleys of southern Wales, with whom they had constant trading contacts. There was a sharp dichotomy between the village that grew so rapidly after 1850 and the surrounding agricultural area, both in terms of employment and the characteristics of the community. Few of the inhabitants of the village regarded themselves as 'country people' and their interests were those of the town dweller; the billiard hall, brass bands, soccer teams and male voice choirs. Many families had relatives in industrial south Wales and during the period between the two wars especially, the Labour Party flourished in an area where Liberalism had previously held sway. Undoubtedly, the whole life of a village such as Dre-fach Felindre was tied up with textile manufacturing and while the industry flourished, so too did a wide range of cultural, social and religious institutions. The same was also true of certain communities in northern Ceredigion where lead and silver were mined and where many immigrant labourers were employed.

Although small, the towns of Ceredigion have always been of importance as markets for extensive hinterlands. The two most important, Aberteifi and Aberystwyth are castle towns that grew around the nucleii of important castles that were built by invaders in order to subjugate the native population. In the Middle Ages castles located near the sea or on navigable waterways were all important for foreign armies. There were quays where soldiers could disembark and where military supplies could be landed. The castles were built on strategic sites and in times of siege, they were assured of supplies by sea. In time, towns grew in the shadows of castle walls and as time progressed and the dangers of war receded the castle towns developed into trading centres of considerable importance as the seas around Wales became important for the pursuit of trade.

From the 12th century until the Civil War in the 17th century Ceredigion and its people were kept in check by the garrisons housed in the two main castles of the area – Aberystwyth and Aberteifi. Aberteifi castle was demolished by Cromwell's army in 1645 and two years later the Aberystwyth castle was reduced to a ruin to prevent it being used by Royalist armies. Of course the Ceredigion of the middle ages and later was largely a rural backwater and the towns, such as they were, were small. In 1565 for instance Aberteifi had no more than 55 houses but by 1831 the census notes that there were 578 houses in the town. Aberystwyth in 1565 had 75 houses but by 1831 it had 712 houses; today it is the largest of Ceredigion's urban centres.

2
ABERTEIFI (CARDIGAN)

The attractive town of Aberteifi, located about a mile and a half upstream of the mouth of the river Teifi, was until the early nineteenth century the most important of Welsh seaports. Its Customs House at one time controlled all shipping and trade from ports and creeks between Abergwaun in the south and Aberarth in the north. It had a thriving shipbuilding industry and well over two hundred vessels were built on the banks of the Teifi, in Aberteifi and a little downstream in the village of Llandudoch. In 1815, Aberteifi possessed no fewer than 314 ships of a total tonnage of 12,554 tons and it was, at the time, the most important of the southern Wales ports, owning seven times as many ships as Caerdydd and three times as many as Abertawe. Its vessels not only plied the Irish Sea and along the coasts of Britain, but sailed further afield to the Mediterranean and the Baltic and across the Atlantic to Canada and the United States of America. Emigrant ships departed frequently for the New World and the settlement at New Cardigan near Fredericton in New Brunswick, for example, remains as a monument to those Aberteifi ships that transported a discontented peasantry to seek a new life in Canada. Even in later times, when Aberteifi itself had ceased to exist as an active seaport, the maritime tradition still lived on and found expression in all quarters of the globe. By the end of the nineteenth century few Aberteifi men sailed in Aberteifi ships but a very large number still went to sea. Many marine engineers serving on liners and tramp steamers the world over were initially trained at an Aberteifi foundry which was originally established to deal with vessels that sailed from the river Teifi. That foundry earned for itself a considerable reputation for its engineers.

The town of Aberteifi owes its existence to its strategic position on the banks of the river Teifi. When Ceredigion was conquered by the Norman, Robert Montgomery, in 1093 he chose a strategic site on the north bank of the river, opposite the village of Llandudoch, for his fortress. The name 'Old Castle Farm' denotes the position of Aberteifi's first castle. This strategic site gave the Norman army easy access to the Irish Sea and inland to the fertile Teifi valley. Later, a permanent castle, half a mile upstream from the 'Old Castle', was built in a commanding position overlooking a bridging point on the river Teifi. The walled settlement of Aberteifi grew around the castle and the town saw much violence in its early years and the Norman invaders were defeated. In 1176 the Lord Rhys held a great meeting at Aberteifi castle; a meeting that has been described as the very first *eisteddfod*. It was proclaimed twelve months in advance and competitors came from all parts of Wales, England, Scotland and Ireland to compete for chairs in poetry and music.

The wide expanse of river below the castle and bridge was to witness the development of a major port with world-wide connections in later centuries. In the Middle Ages there was much river traffic, especially in timber and despite the fact that Bae Ceredigion was a notorious centre of pirate activity, there was a great deal of trade with Ireland. To invaders, Aberteifi was crucial, not only as a strategic point for the domination of Ceredigion but also as a trading centre through which activities could be controlled and supervised and by 1199 when Aberteifi received its first charter it was already an important centre of trade. A weekly Saturday market, that still continues to attract people from a wide area, was held as early as 1227.

Until the sixteenth century, Aberteifi was a small walled market town with some river traffic, but as a result of the Act of Union which brought political stability to Wales, maritime trade increased rapidly. Navigation Acts were passed in an endeavour to increase trade and piracy which was so rife along the coast of Bae Ceredigion was suppressed and steps were taken to encourage sea fisheries. The machinery for the collection of customs revenue was reorganised and the stage was set for a considerable expansion of maritime activity. It was this great expansion that was to ensure the development of Aberteifi as the most important of Welsh ports. In Tudor times it was above all else a herring fishing port, but the herring became such an important item of trade that English, Irish, French and Spanish ships came to Aberteifi to take away the harvest of the sea. Gradually, Aberteifi men began to take a far greater interest in seafaring and by the dawn of the eighteenth century, the port had a substantial merchant fleet. Salmon and herrings, Cilgerran slate and oak bark for the tanning industry, ale and corn were exported in substantial quantities and a whole variety of goods ranging from Spanish oranges to cooking utensils, and from coal to building materials were all imported. By the end of the eighteenth century, Aberteifi had attained a position of great importance as a port and distribution centre to an extensive hinterland.

With this explosion in trade, the demand for ships increased and an important shipbuilding industry developed on the north bank of the Teifi below the bridge. Industry was attracted to Aberteifi; there were tinplate works at nearby Llechryd and in the town itself, substantial brickworks whose products were widely exported were built. Added to these industries, were those concerned with maritime trade. In 1837 the town had four blacksmiths while the Bridge End Foundry and Bailey's Foundry were principally concerned with producing essentials for ships. The area around the Mwldan Brook was the industrial centre of Aberteifi; it had a shipyard, brickyard, a foundry and a workshop responsible for providing pulley blocks for ships. The town also supported at least three ropemakers and three sailmakers together with two anchor smiths and as befitted an important sea port it had as many as fifty-five public houses.

But, in addition to being an important sea port, Aberteifi was above all else a market town that catered for the needs of a substantial region. Its public buildings, erected in 1860, accommodated a Corn, Meat, Wool and Skin Market in addition to a Guildhall. Its Goose Fair was renowned and its Barley Saturday at the end of April still remains an important day in the calendar of the farming community. Originally, Barley Saturday marked the end of the sowing season on the farms of southern Ceredigion and north Pembrokeshire. It was the date when cattle were allowed to remain out in the fields at night but the highlight of the day was traditionally a parade of stallions through the main streets of the town. This was an opportunity for farmers to select and reserve a stallion to visit their farms, for the quality of draught horses was crucial to the success of husbandry. At the November fair of *Calan Gaeaf* farmers again came to Aberteifi in order to engage labour for the coming year. Those looking for employment stood in one of the side streets of the town to be interviewed by prospective employers. An agreement between farmer and servant was sealed with the clap of hands, possibly with the passing of a sovereign to the servant. Once that agreement had been made, it was considered a very serious breach of contract for the servant to withdraw or make an agreement with another farmer who had offered better wages and conditions.

3
ST DOGMAELS (LLANDUDOCH) AND THE SEINE NETSMEN

Dominated by a ruined Benedictine Abbey, the village of Llandudoch although no more than a mile downstream of Aberteifi, has nevertheless a character of its own. It is a riverside village, a little upstream of the dangerous bar at the mouth of the Teifi and traditionally, river activity has dominated the life of the community. Above all, the capture of the salmon and its close relative, the sewin or sea trout has been all important in the economy of the village. The last of those seine netsmen gave up fishing in August 1999, although attempts have been made to revive the activity.

The shore seine is widely used around Britain, particularly in river estuaries, and is a simply constructed, plain wall of netting two hundred yards or more in length and of a depth suitable to the water in which it is used. It is important that the net extends as far as possible from the surface of the water to the bottom and it should stand as vertical as possible in the water. The head-rope is fitted with corks or plastic floats and the foot-rope weighted with lead or stones. The net is carefully stowed on the flat transom of a small boat. One of the crew stands ashore holding a rope attached to the end of the net. The boat is then rowed out from the shore into the stream on a semi-circular course, with the net being paid out over the stern. When all the net has been shot, the boat returns to the shore. The crew then lands, the boat is made fast and the net hauled in. The landing place is usually downstream of the shoreman but the net is occasionally shot upstream if the boat is equipped with an outboard motor. The hauling of the net is rapid and smooth, and the two ends of the net are brought close together 'thus making a narrow bag of the middle of the enclosed space, where the fish are concentrated and can be hauled ashore. The foot-rope is hauled faster than the headline, thus making a more pronounced bag of the centre of the net.' The whole net is drawn in; the salmon or sewin caught in its mesh are killed with the knocker and the net has to be re-arranged on the boat transom ready for the next shot.

Seine nets are used in the Teifi estuary below the village of Llandudoch for catching salmon and sea trout. The *rhwydau sân*, as they are known locally, measure 200 yards in length, have a mesh of 2 inches from knot to knot and are 12 feet in depth. Rowing boats equipped with outboard motors are used; in the past the boats were referred to by the fishermen as *llestri sân* (seine vessels).

Undoubtedly, seine net fishing has been well known on the Teifi for many centuries. George Owen, writing in 1603, for example, describes the *'great store'* of salmon *'as allso of sueings, mullettes and botchers, taken in the said River neere St dogmells in a sayne net after everye tyde'*. Until the present century, salmon and sewin fishing in the spring and summer and herring fishing in the autumn and winter seem to have been the main occupation of the inhabitants of Llandudoch. 'It affords employment', said one nineteenth century author, 'to such of the inhabitants that are not engaged in agricultural pursuits.' It is difficult to estimate the extent of seine net fishing of the Teifi in the past, but in 1884 there were sixty-two licensed netsmen on the Teifi and large quantities of salmon and sewin were taken. During the summer of 1883 'as much as half a ton of salmon was caught in the lower reaches of the river and sent to London and other places in one day.'

During the course of the present century and particularly since 1939, there has been a steady decrease in the number of seine net fishermen operating in the Teifi estuary. In 1939 there were thirteen boats, each one manned by a team of five fishermen; today the number has decreased to six boats, each manned by four men only. In the 1920s, each team consisted of seven fishermen and it has been estimated that twenty boats were engaged in seine net fishing at the time. The twenty-four full-time fishermen of Llandudoch were all members of the 'St Dogmaels Seine Net Fishermen's Association', whose headquarters were at the Netpool Inn in the village.

In the seine netting pools of the Teifi it is believed that if a parson or preacher is seen on the shore, it is an omen of ill luck. In 1965 an old ceremony of blessing the fishing harvest was revived on the Netpool at Llandudoch. Many of the fishermen believe that the poor salmon seasons experienced since then are due almost entirely to the revival of this religious ceremony and that the presence of gentlemen of the cloth at that ceremony has contributed to the absence of fish from the river. Someone appearing on the bank in red clothes is also an omen of bad luck, but someone dressed in white would be very welcome. The cry of a bird, known locally as the 'Welsh parrot', (probably a Red Shank) that screeches the words *Dim byd, dim byd* (nothing, nothing) also signifies that that particular fishing session will be without a catch, particularly if that bird flies across the river and over the fishing team. It is also considered bad luck to grasp the *cnocer* from the bottom of the boat before the net has been hauled in. Here amongst the netsmen of the Teifi estuary, there are customs, practices and beliefs that may be traced back many centuries.

4
TEIFI-SIDE AND ITS CORACLES

The Teifi valley between Castellnewydd Emlyn and Aberteifi is a green, well-wooded area with lush pastures in the valley floor, beautiful waterfalls, well designed bridges and the general appearance of having been established for centuries. Here, on the gently sloping valley sides, were the homes of the aristocracy who owned many acres of land and 'the squires of Tivyside' exercised a considerable influence on the social, cultural and political life of western Wales.

Here too, many craftsmen practised their trade. There were many corn mills, such as the one at Cenarth, woollen mills, tanneries, tinplate works and sawmills that utilised the waters of the Teifi to drive machinery. The abundance of timber in the Teifi valley and its tributaries also gave rise to notable woodland industries, the most important being that of bowl turning and spoon carving. The village of Aber-cuch was a well-known centre of woodland craftsmanship and as recently as 1930 there were at least seven families in the village who were entirely dependent on the craft. There were also others who worked on a part-time basis combining farming or some other occupation with a certain amount of bowl turning. The fame of Aber-cuch as a centre of remarkable craftsmanship had spread far beyond the boundaries of Wales and even as recently as 1935, the prospects of the industry were regarded as excellent. A Guide issued in that year says 'a growing recognition of the aesthetic beauty of the well turned bowl is creating a new demand for the products of the wood turner'; yet twenty-five years later all the craftsmen had disappeared. They disappeared because of the availability of mass-produced goods and also because Aber-cuch turners had been unable to find apprentices to learn a trade that demands great craftsmanship and long experience before full competence is achieved. The woods of Cwm Cuch which not very long were alive with the sound of the woodman's axe are silent; the doors of the once busy workshops are closed and the buzzing of a dozen pole lathes has ceased. For the first time in its long history Aber-cuch has become a quiet village with little to show of its past glory as a centre of woodland artistry.

Another important aspect of the turner's work was the making of wooden spoons. In the past, wooden spoons were used in Welsh households for a great variety of purposes. Small 10 inch spoons were always required for eating *cawl*, that unique broth of bacon, leeks and other vegetables, the recipe for which seems to have been limited to the western counties of Wales. *Cawl* still remains extremely popular in Welsh farmhouses and many people will not eat it with anything but a wooden spoon. The spoon carvers, in addition to making broth spoons, also made a variety of large spoons and ladles ranging from butter scoops for use in the dairy to kitchen spatulas and stirrers. All these were made by hand using a few simple tools.

The wooden spoon, despite its simplicity, has been an article of great importance in Welsh peasant life. Although many villages had their full time craftsmen, the carving of wooden spoons as a pastime in the long winter evenings also became very popular on Welsh farms. Some of the spoons were undoubtedly designed to be used but from the seventeenth to the end of the nineteenth century the highly decorated spoon presented by the maker as a token of love became a very common feature of rural life. These were not designed to be used and most of them were very intricate and elaborate in design, with slotted handles, chain links and carved patterns and initials. The aim, wherever possible, seems to have been to carve an intricate pattern out of a single piece of wood, and since the donor of the love spoon was also the maker he tried to emphasise the feeling and care that had gone into its making by elaborating the design as much as possible. The origin of the custom is very obscure but, undoubtedly, in remote country districts where entertainment was at a premium, young men carved their tokens of love to beguile the tedium of the long, dark winter evenings and to prove their dexterity.

Although the Teifi valley has no bowl turners today, a member of one of the best known families who had been turners for at least seven generations still practices a woodland craft in a sawmill on the banks of the Teifi. Here, it is not the decorative tableware and the utilitarian dairy utensils that are produced at the sawmills but tool handles and rakes which are still in demand in all parts of the country.

Cenarth in particular, but also Aber-cuch, Llechryd and Cilgerran, was noted for its coracles and although coracle fishing has virtually disappeared in the non-tidal reaches of the river above Llechryd bridge, one may still see the occasional pair of coracles drifting with the flow of the water, a net between them, practising an age-old technique. The coracle fishermen were described a hundred years ago as a numerous class bound together by a strong *esprit de corps* and from a long and undisturbed enjoyment of that particular mode of fishing they have come to look on the river almost as their own and to regard with extreme jealousy any sign of interference with what they consider their rights'. The coracle fishermen of the Teifi were, therefore, almost a closed community and custom dictated that only fishermen from four river-side villages were allowed to fish in the river. The four villages concerned were Cilgerran, Cenarth, Aber-cuch and Llechryd. The river was divided into four sections; the fishermen from one of those four villages having the sole right to fish in those sections of the river. Each section was known as a *bwrw* (cast), and each *bwrw* was divided into three parts, each of which was called a *traill* (trawl). At Cilgerran, for example, the principal trawl *(y draill)* was that side of the river nearest the village; the second trawl *(yr ail draill)* signified the middle of the river and *yr hawel* or *tu'r dre* signified a third trawl on the opposite side of the river from the principal trawl. According to local tradition, each of the eight casts belonging to Cilgerran coracle men had its own characteristics. These are expressed in a doggerel verse passed down over the many generations.

Bwrw byr hyfryd, Brocen ddryslyd
Gwegrydd lana, Nantyffil lwma.
Crow'n rhoddi, Pwll du'n pallu
Bwmbwll yn hela, Draill fach yn dala.

(Lovely Bwrw byr, complex Brocen,
Cleanest Gwegrydd, poorest Nantyffil.
When Crow gives, Pwll du refuses
When one hunts at Bwmbell, you may catch at Draill fach.)

Each of the main casts had minor casts to them but there were also seventeen other minor casts that were not attached to the principal *bwrws.* 'In or about the month of April,' said a writer in 1867, 'the town crier used to convene by a public cry a meeting of all the fishermen. Formerly,' he adds, 'none were permitted to fish in that part of the Teivi which borders on the confines of this parish, save those who had previously been admitted burgesses of the ancient borough of Cilgerran, so that the river being entirely monopolised by them, strangers were effectually excluded from participating in the fishery'. At the annual April meeting of the fishermen, the turns or casts for slips of paper on which were written the names of the eight principal casts and of the minor casts were deposited in a hat. Each fisherman, in turn, picked out a slip, and whatever name or position might be written on that slip would be his station for the opening night of the salmon fishing season. This arrangement, of course, 'only held good for the first night, for he that would have the best chance on the first trawl . . . would be the last on the next cast the following night, and so on, until he had gone through all the sub-divisions in each *bwrw.* If a fisherman should absent himself from his station on any one night, no one could take his place, for the allocation of casts was very rigidly enforced at all times. The starting point of every station was termed *pen bwrw* (the head of the cast), where the coracles were placed in order of precedence. The two leading coracles were required to be with their keels on the ground, in the same position as when on the water, with the paddle resting on the seat. If this rule was not adhered to, the owners of the leading coracles were deprived of their trawl.

These rigid rules of precedence and privilege were undoubtedly framed by the fishermen themselves and were invaluable in that disputes were avoided. They were oral laws passed down from father to son in a closely knit village community and were practised with little variation by the coracle men of Llechryd, Abercuch and Cenarth, as well as those of Cilgerran. Before the eighteen sixties, the closed season for salmon fishing on the Teifi was also a matter of unwritten law rather than of legislation and it extended from August to February. One fisherman in each village was responsible for locking up the coracles during the closed season.

The eighteen sixties saw the end of the rigid rules of precedence that had been practised on the river from time immemorial. At Cilgerran for example, 'before a person has any certainty of a draw he must need place himself at the starting point and then remain with his coracle from the morning till the evening sets in and the darkness enables him to spread his net to advantage, and even this patient watching does not always now secure a first position. In fact there is no regulation whatever adhered to, everybody scrambles for the first chance, and everybody spreads his net wherever he thinks it likely to obtain a fish'. Nevertheless, even today, this is not quite true, for among the half dozen coracles that operate in Cilgerran gorge, vestiges of the older system still remain. The first coracle on the river during a fishing session is still referred to as *yr ergyd*; the second as *yr ail draill* and the third as *y trydydd* and only three pairs are allowed on the river at the same time. Fishing is still practised in strict rotation and the first net may not enter the water a second time until the first trawl by all the other coracles is complete.

5
CASTELLNEWYDD EMLYN

Strictly speaking, the town of Castellnewydd Emlyn is not in Ceredigion but in the county of Caerfyrddin. The ancient borough of Adpar or Trehedyn however, on the right hand bank of the Teifi, across the well designed bridge is of considerable importance in that it returned its own member of parliament and had its own port-reeve and two bailiffs. It was also a market town of some importance with a series of seasonal animal fairs. The folds for the animals were located at the side of the steep hill of Bryndioddef and the pace of the horses offered for sale was demonstrated by running them across the bridge and back again. As befitted an important market town, the borough of Adpar had a large number of inns and it was in one of these inns – the Salutation, that events leading to one of the last duels in Wales were to unfold. In 1814, two men by the name of Heslop and Beynon after a drunken orgy in the Salutation vied for the favours of a barmaid at the inn. Things deteriorated and it was decided to fight a duel with pistols on the banks of the Teifi. Heslop was killed and was buried at nearby Llandyfriog Church where his gravestone still bears the sentiment 'Alas poor Heslop'.

The Adpar bank of the river Teifi was the location of a number of industrial enterprises that utilised the water of the rapidly flowing stream to turn mill machinery. The most important of the enterprises was a woollen mill that produced flannel and blankets and knitting yarn that were sold at local markets. There was also a fish weir for the capture of migratory salmon above the bridge until the last quarter of the 19th century. In Adpar too, was founded the first printing press in Wales. It was established near the river bank by Isaac Carter who published the first book in 1719. One of Carter's first publications was a song sheet cursing 'the Old Master-Tobacco', but by 1724 he had moved his centre of operations from Adpar to Caerfyrddin where his business flourished for some years.

Adpar today is not much of a town and there is little to signify that this straggling village once enjoyed borough status. It is now very much a suburb of the adjacent market town of Castellnewydd Emlyn. That town seems to come alive on Friday, its traditional market day. Its spring and autumn fair were always important events in the farming calendar and again, as befitted an important market town, it also possessed a large number of taverns. In the middle ages the town was known as Dinas Emlyn and its early castle, built on a hillock dominated a curve on the river Teifi, occupied a strategic position. It was rebuilt by Rhys ap Thomas, an ally of Henry Tudor and this gave the town that grew in its shadows the name of 'New' castle. The town straddled a bridging point on the river but it also straddled the two counties – Ceredigion and Caerfyrddin.

Situated on the Ceredigion side of the river was an important stately home within half a mile of the river bank. This was Cilgwyn, now a somewhat sinister looking Victorian mansion and once the home of the very important Lloyd family. One of the family was a naval captain in the 18th century who, unfortunately, lost his ship. At the same time a friend of his, a Captain Braithwaite had also lost his ship and in a fit of bravado the two captains decided to toss a coin to determine which estate had to be sold in order to buy two new ships. Captain Lloyd won, but unfortunately his new ship was destroyed by fire. When he died in 1801, he willed the whole Cilgwyn estate to his friend, who was by then Admiral Braithwaite. The Admiral's descendants, the Fitzwilliams, continued to occupy Cilgwyn until the 1950s and some members of the family still live in the Castellnewydd Emlyn area.

6
LLANBEDR PONT STEFFAN

To many, the town of Llanbedr Pont Steffan is a centre of fashion and shopping that draws its clientele from an extensive area. This is a mere extension of its ancient role for Llanbedr Pont Steffan, from when it was awarded its first Charter in 1284, it has always served as the most important town in the Teifi valley. Strategically located astride a bridging point, Llanbedr Pont Steffan had its Norman castle demolished in 1187 by Owain Gwynedd. It was an important ecclesiastical centre that supplied many fighting men for the Crusades but it was really as a market town that it developed. In 1284, Rhys ap Meredydd was granted the right to hold a weekly market in the town and over the centuries as many as eight fairs a year were held there in addition to the weekly market. By 1800, all these were regarded as extremely rough and rowdy affairs, characterised by drunkenness and violence. No wonder the stocks in the High Street and the whipping post in front of the Town Hall were well utilised facilities especially in the 18th century when the peace of the town was frequently disturbed by what was described as 'bloody frays and assaults'.

Of course, the Llanbedr Pont Steffan magistrates were not averse to handing out the severest of sentences to those who had transgressed. For this town was, until the end of the 18th century, a feudal town ruled by a rod of iron by a local aristocracy, many of whom were harsh and pitiless in their treatment of those that appeared before them. The elegant mansions of Brynhywel, Maesyfelin and Peterwell were occupied by resident squires, some good but many bad, who ruled the town and its environs like desert despots. The Lloyds of Maesyfelin and Peterwell, some of whose members held high office and were leaders of the Royalist cause in the Civil War, became pretty notorious in the 18th century. After the Civil War they accumulated great wealth and acquired for themselves Peterwell, the most beautiful of all Ceredigion stately homes. Before 1700, when Peterwell obtained Maesyfelin, some notoriety had accompanied the Maesyfelin family. Samuel Pritchard, the son of the best known 18th century poet, the Vicar

Rhys Pritchard of Llandovery, was in love with one of the daughters of Maesyfelin and is said to have been murdered by servants of Peterwell and his body thrown into the river Tywi. This prompted the vicar to write:

'The curse of God on Maes-y-felin fall
And every stone in its detested wall'

Within a few years Maesyfelin was in decline and local lore maintained that the vicar's curse was also passed on to the new mansion of Peterwell and its occupants.

The most notorious of all the Lloyds of Peterwell was Herbert Lloyd, baronet, magistrate and member of parliament, a bully, schemer and corrupt despot who became a terror to the town and surrounding countryside.

'No crime seems to have been too base no treachery too great for this great squire and magistrate,' says a writer in 1900.

The story of Cae Siôn Philip (John Philip's field) is well known. The farm property adjoined the Peterwell estate and the baronet was determined to possess it. On failing to buy it, he arranged for a valuable ram to be let down the chimney at night. He then prosecuted the hapless John Philip for sheep stealing. Sir Herbert's power as a magistrate and member of parliament and the fear he inspired in any who might court his favours to assist the alleged culprit, ensured a verdict of guilty and John Philip was executed at Aberteifi. Sir Herbert was a great gambler, however, and it was in a gambling den that he eventually met his match, losing all his wealth. The estate at Peterwell was finished and a far more benign family, the Harfords of Blair Castle near Bristol, took over the estate. But the Peterwell mansion was deteriorating rapidly and a new house, Falcondale, was built to accommodate the family. The Harfords were certainly the benefactors of late 18th and early 19th century Llanbedr Pont Steffan and they gave generously to the building of a new Town Hall and provided land for the development of St David's College.

That college, now a constituent of the University of Wales, was founded in 1827 by Bishop Burgess of St David's to secure better training for those entering the Anglican priesthood. Well before its foundation, a scheme had been prepared for setting up a college in the remote village of Llanddewi Brefi, but the presentation of a site in Llanbedr Pont Steffan by J. S. Harford decided the ultimate location of the college. The government provided a grant of £6000 to which King George IV when Prince Regent contributed £1000 from the private purse. The University of Oxford and Cambridge contributed £200 each, the squire of Falcondale gave £1000 and the squire of Derry Ormond £500. The foundation stone was laid by Bishop Burgess in 1822 and the elegant main building, an Oxford college in miniature, was opened in 1827. In 1852, the college was granted a charter empowering it to award the degree of BD and in 1865 a further charter empowered the conferring of a BA degree was granted.

Llanbedr Pont Steffan, like many another country town, had the service, craft and industries concerned with catering for the needs of its hinterland. It had woollen mills, one of which in the mid 18th century was producing the highly complex double-woven tapestry cloth so closely associated with the Welsh Woollen Industry in the 1950s and 1960s. It had its leather tannery, its blacksmiths, saddlers, hatters, bootmakers, carpenters and others who fulfilled the needs of a rural population. Indeed, Llanbedr Pont Steffan was truly a market town and was also at one time, but to a lesser extent than Tregaron, an important centre for the dispatch of animals on the hoof to English markets. Street names such as Drovers' Road and the multiplicity of inns; the Nag's Head, Swan, Star, Drovers, Greyhound, Ship, Three Horseshoes, Crown, Green Dragon, and Black Lion all point to the importance of the town as a centre of rural activity.

7
TREGARON

Tregaron, small though it may be, has always been the most Welsh of Welsh towns. It did not have its origins in the building of a medieval castle like Aberystwyth, Aberteifi or Llanbedr Pont Steffan; it was never a feudal town dominated by an Anglicised class of landed gentry like Llanbedr Pont Steffan. Here in the upper reaches of the Teifi valley, there were no large estates and there was no domination of the native population by aristocratic families that forced allegiance and servitude. This was, and still is an essentially Welsh town, a valley market town that owed its origin and growth to its strategic location as a centre for widely differing agricultural communities. Here were the relatively prosperous farmers who lived in the well cultivated Teifi valley while to the north lies Cors Caron, a fertile plain when drained. To the south, the Teifi meanders through a broad, long settled valley. Here, farms are prosperous, the land is fertile and dairy farming, together with the cultivation of cereal crops, has always been of importance. Here too, were small industrial undertakings, such as woollen and corn mills while in the small valley hamlets such as Llangybi and Betws Bledrws were the workshops of several craftsmen who supplied the needs of the farming population.

This green and pleasant landscape contrasts sharply with the hill country of Mynydd Bach to the west. This cradle of Welsh Calvinistic Methodism was dominated by hundreds of very small peasant farms whose inhabitants were well known for many hand crafts such as spoon carving and embroidery that were so characteristic of the material culture of isolated rural communities where entertainment was at a premium. Many of the smallholdings around hill villages such as Penuwch, Swyddffynnon and Bethania originated in the squatter houses of a peasantry whose ambition was to own a few acres of land that they could call their own, in an attempt to be self sufficient. This is the land of the *tyddynwr*, the smallholder; of home made homes and of rural skills amongst a poor people who depended on their own resources and the dexterity of their hands for the means of life. For them too, Tregaron is the main market town.

East of the river Teifi, however, is a forbidden land of dark mountains, hidden river gullies and a harsh unyielding environment. This is a land of sheep and few people; a land of extensive ranches and the ranches of the past were rich and autocratic. It is no coincidence that the most famous of all Welsh robbers – Twm Siôn Cati (Thomas Jones 1530-1609) whose exploits have been celebrated in song and pantomime was a substantial sheep farmer in the hill land beyond Tregaron. By tradition, the farmers of the hills visit Tregaron on market or fair days but the country around the remote chapel of Soar y Mynydd and stretches to the upper reaches of the Tywi and to Abergwesyn is a secret land, sometimes sinister and forbidding. 'Some of these sheep farms were very extensive' said Ieuan Gwynedd Jones 'and their owners resembled barons and, indeed, as has been the case in the past, robber barons, and the landowners who occupied their miserable hovels were like retainers of old. The funerals when they carried their dead to the parish church tended to be like their weddings, noisy, strange and rather intimidating.

To many widely differing communities in north-east Ceredigion, Tregaron was and still is the market and fair town. Dominated by a large church and an even larger Methodist chapel, it still has its weekly market. The annual Ffair Garon, once regarded as a rough, bruising occasion, was held for three days for the sale of poultry, pigs, cattle and horses. The sheep fairs held in May and June and two hiring fairs in November, point to the importance of Tregaron as a frontier town. There was also a multiplicity of inns and taverns despite the stranglehold of Calvinistic Methodism.

Tregaron was one of the main gathering depots for the drovers and their vast herds of cattle, flocks of sheep and even geese that walked in noisy processions to the markets of Barnet, Watford and other places in south-east England. Many Tregaron men were drovers and many accumulated vast wealth from the hard task of driving unwilling animals on a cross country trek of hundreds of miles. In some treks they avoided all toll-gates and the drovers themselves acted as unofficial postmen, news carriers and even as bankers to the population. Indeed some important banks – Bank of the Black Ox, Bank of the Black Sheep, and others, had their origins in the droving trade that was of considerable importance in the life of Wales until the advent of the railways and improved roads. Tregaron reigned supreme in the droving trade.

As befitted its location in a sheep rearing region, Tregaron was, in the past, heavily involved in the manufacture of woollen socks. The area had a number of water-driven woollen mills but it was better known as a centre for the manufacture of hosiery. It was, of course, a domestic industry where men and children, as well as the women, were involved in the knitting of woollen socks that were sold in the market and taken to the industrial valleys of southern Wales by a number of local hosiery dealers.

Dominating the modest square of Tregaron is a statue of the town's most illustrious resident. He was Henry Richard (1812-1888) the 'Apostle of Peace', Minister, Secretary of the Peace Society and a member of parliament who contributed much to the political life of Victorian Britain.

Aberporth, c.1890.

New Quay from post card loaned by Mr. Steve Rowson, c.1906.

The Smack Albatross on Llangrannog beach, c.1890.

Butter working, Maesllyn, 1969
(Mr & Mrs J. Thomas).

Printing butter.

Extracting air from churn.

Sheep shearing.

A sheep shearing gang on a north Ceredigion farm.

A reaper-binder that became common on the farm, between 1910 and 1939.

A reaper that preceeded the binder for harvesting corn on Ceredigion farms.

The hay harvest that depended heavily on co-operation between neighbours.

Stooking (stacaro) *corn sheares on a Teifi valley farm, 1968.*

Ben Evans lip-worker Penuwch, 1970.

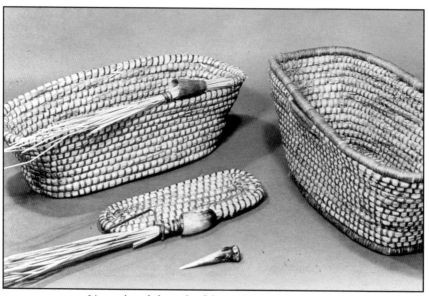
Lip work and the tools of the trade – Penuwch, 1970.

Constructing field ricks (Teise on Sopine) *Evan John Jones Nantybach, Llangrannog, c.1952.*

Llanrhystud Woollen Mill, 1934.

Woollen Mill, Tal-y-bont, 1936.

Maesllyn. The weaver is Tom Rees of Coed-y-bryn, c.1965.

Charcoal burning, Tal-y-bont, c.1936.

Clog sole making. Itinerant Cloggery at Tal-y-bont, c.1920.

Tyring a wooden wheel, Cardigan, c.1977.

Shrinking the tyre.

42

Peat cutting, Tregaron area, c.1980.

Llanybydder horse fair, c.1940.

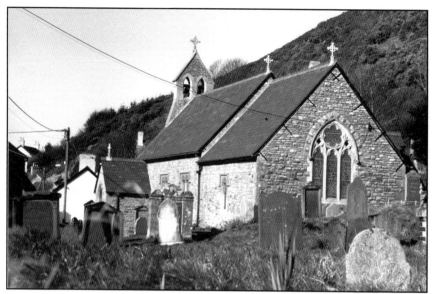

The church of St. Carannog. Rebuilt in 1885 on site of 6th century church.

Sunday school at Penmorfa chapel, 1918.

Penmorfa Presbyterian Church. Built 1758. Renovated 1938.

Soar-y-mynydd, Presbyterian chapel, 2000.

Tre'r-ddôl. A Westleyan chapel converted to a museum.

Aberaeron.

The S.S. Aberporth *owned in the village and wrecked soon after its purchase in 1904.*

River Teifi at Aberteifi (Cardigan).

Annie *of Aberteifi (D.V.T. Davies).*

*A Teifi ship-building yard at Mwldan
(D.V.T. Davies).*

ESCAPES FROM LINER WRECK
CREW RESCUED BY BREECHES BUOY

The Liner Herefordshire *wrecked off
Ynys Aberteifi in 1934.*

8
THE COASTAL VILLAGES

Ceredigion has a long indented coastline with numerous bays and headlands and it was almost inevitable that the county should have developed a maritime tradition that can be traced back to prehistoric times. In-shore and river fishing, the transporting of both goods and people by sea have always been vital elements in the heritage of Ceredigion. Since maritime occupations were so well established for so many centuries, it is only natural that in those communities where seafaring was of importance that they should have developed their own character and personality. Many of the coastal settlements of Ceredigion were, in effect, self-contained communities that looked outwards towards the sea, and the oceans dominated the lives and thinking of its inhabitants.

Much of the early history of Ceredigion was shaped by invaders who came by sea. For thousands of years before the arrival of the Romans, traders and settlers utilised the open sea routes of Atlantic Britain. Settlers came from lands across the sea, bringing with them their own ways of life and a Celtic tongue that still flourishes in the county. In later centuries, Christianity came to western Britain by sea, and the well-travelled seas around south-western Wales became the highways of Celtic missionaries who brought with them the ascetic austerity of the Celtic church. To those wandering missionaries, the sea constituted a highway rather than a barrier and many of the religious settlements that they established at such places as Llangrannog and Ferwig, Llansanffraid and Llanina were fairly close to sandy beaches where the frail vessels that transported them could be safely landed.

Much of the maritime activity of the Middle Ages was linked to the buildings and defence of Norman and English castles. At Aberystwyth for example, following Edward I's campaign against Llywelyn ap Gruffudd in 1277, it was decided that a fortified borough with a large castle should be established near that point where the rivers Ystwyth and Rheidol converged before flowing to the sea. This small estuary was conveniently protected by a shingle spit known as *Y Ro Fawr* and with overland transport to Aberystwyth in those troubled times being both difficult and dangerous, it was here that most of the men and materials employed in the construction of the castle were landed. Most of the fortresses in Ceredigion could be supplied from the sea if besieged from the land and undoubtedly foreign ships were often seen along the coast of Ceredigion. Few ships were from Wales and Giraldus Cambrensis on his tour in the twelfth century remarked upon the almost total absence of native shipping: the medieval Cardi was no sailor. He did fish a little, however, although he never ventured far from the sight of land and Aberystwyth, in particular, became a very important centre of herring fishing in the 13th century. 'God provided more fish than ever before' said *Brut y Tywysogion* and since the number of herrings caught were far too many for the population of the borough and surrounding countryside, more and more salted herrings and smoked herrings were exported, principally to Ireland. But almost all the exports were transported in Irish and English vessels. It was only very slowly that the natives of Ceredigion began to take an interest in something more than merely capturing herrings along the coast but then they too, started to take an interest in sailing to distant lands. By the eighteenth century, the virtual monopoly of sea trade by foreign mariners was being broken and the natives of Ceredigion were taking more and more interest in commercial activity. New coastal settlements developed on hitherto uninhabited creeks and seafaring developed into a distinct and separate occupation while a very important shipbuilding industry developed in the creeks and beaches of the county. Maritime trade became almost an epidemic and hundreds of sailing vessels were owned in the coastal villages and towns with the heyday of activity being in the first half of the nineteenth century. Most of the commodities that the communities could not provide for themselves were brought in by sea and smacks, schooners, brigs and barques brought in coal and culm from southern Wales, wine from Bordeaux and crockery from Chester. There were regular sailings from ports such as Aberystwyth to North America, taking emigrants to the land of opportunity and promise. Maritime activity in Ceredigion before 1914 was not confined to one or two members of a community located on the coast, but it was all embracing. Ceinewydd is an example 'par excellence' of a maritime community.

Further south, the coastal villages of Aber-porth, Tresaith and Llangrannog were also very active maritime communities. Llangrannog is located at the mouth of a small rivulet, the Hawen, that flows through a gorge-like valley with sharply rising hills on both flanks of the village and cutting down to a minimum the contact between the village and its rural hinterland. Like so many other Welsh coastal villages, the settlement was founded by a Celtic missionary of the sixth century to whom the sea was a highway rather than a barrier. Although the original village of Llangrannog was located near the church of St Caranoc, half a mile away from the sea, by the mid-eighteenth century a second nucleation had developed on the foreshore and by 1800 that 'Beach Village' had become far more important than the earlier 'Church Village'. It was an important centre of shipbuilding. The vessels which ranged in size from the sloop 'Linnet' of 9 tons burthen in 1824, to the deep-sea brig 'Anne Catherine' of 211 tons burthen in 1859 were constructed on Llangrannog beach. The village in the nineteenth century had a number of warehouses including one described as Y Storws Lestri (The earthenware warehouse) where crockery, bricks, roofing and drainage tiles from Buckley were stored for sale. There were also two extensive coal and culm yards and three sets of limekilns.

As recently as 1900 almost every male inhabitant of the village of Llangrannog was associated with seafaring either as sailors or fishermen or as merchants associated with the import and sale of sea-borne goods.

Aber-porth, like the open beach at Penbryn a mile to the north, was a subsidiary landing creek to the port of Aberteifi in the sixteenth century. The requirements of the fishing industry – salt for preserving, nets for casting and boats – were brought from Ireland. Located at the mouth of the Howni and Gilwen brooks in a sheltered location, the village of Aber-porth developed rapidly in the late seventeenth and early eighteenth centuries as local people began to take part and show an interest in maritime trade. By the mid-nineteenth century a substantial number of vessels were owned by village families and although Aber-porth did not develop as a centre of shipbuilding, it was a very active port. The northernmost of the two beaches at Aber-porth, known as *Traeth y Dyffryn* or *Traeth y Llongau* (the Ship Beach) is a narrow mouthed, gently shelving beach that penetrates deeply into the river valley. It provided a safe, sheltered anchorage for vessels and on its southern shore, limekilns, coalyards and warehouses were constructed.

One of the best known activities of Aber-porth was herring fishing and the village together with Nefyn in Gwynedd, was the principal herring fishing port of Wales. The industry persisted until the beginning of the First World War and heavy rowing boats of 25 feet to 30 feet long and equipped with sails were used. Each boat was manned by a crew of from five to eight and each member of the crew had four or five nets. Two methods of fishing were adopted at Aber-porth – drifting *(drifio)* and netting *(tranio)*. In drifting, a number of nets could be attached together to form a long wall of gill netting and a boat would drift with the tide in search of fish.

The boat with nets attached, drifted as far as the mouth of the Teifi on the ebb returning to Aber-porth and beyond, hopefully catching herrings on the flood. The net was usually attached to a buoy and considerable skill was needed to keep the rapidly drifting boat at right angles to the net.

The other method of fishing was with set nets. Each net, approximately 20 feet deep, was fitted with cork floats *(bwyau corc)* with a bottom rope weighted with a series of round beach pebbles. Each pebble, known as a *collten* (pl. *collte*) was wrapped in a piece of rag attached to the bottom rope. It was important that the net stood upright in the water and considerable skill was necessary in preparing the weighted bottom line *(meino)*. To set the net, a pair of anchors was necessary to keep it in the correct fishing position although a net could be equipped with one anchor leaving the other end free to move with the current.

Setting *(tranio)* was carried out at a number of specific locations in the bay at Aber-porth. Each setting position had a specific name

– Trân Cribach, Trân Croes-y-Traeth, Trân Fath Garreg, Trân Dŵr Nel, Trân Ogo Fraith and Trân y Llety. As in other districts, herrings were counted by the meise *(mwys)*, a measure consisting of five hundred fish. The hundred, *cant fawr*, consisted of 120 herrings and the usual method of counting was to count two score of the fish and throwing one fish aside as a tally. After counting five score herring, another one was thrown aside to denote a hundred. A meise therefore consisted of 120 x 5 herring (600) + 15 warp (the herrings thrown aside to keep a tally of hundreds) = 620 herrings. When sharing out a catch the herrings were counted in threes, a measure known as *mwrw* or *bwrw*. Two herrings were taken in one hand and one in the other and this was repeated forty times to produce a hundred *(cant)*. The catch was shared out equally with a share for each member of the crew, a share for the boat, a share for the net and a share for the owner of the boat.

In coastal communities, fresh herring was a favourite food, but it was considered important that the eyes were red and bright to denote freshness. If the eyes were dull and grey, then the fish was stale and could not be consumed. Fish that had already spawned were not in demand and many fishermen threw those back into the sea or used them as bait in long lining. The fishermen either sold the catch to fish merchants (carriers) to sell in the surrounding countryside. Alternatively they sold directly to farmers and others who came to the beach with carts to await the returning fishermen. Unlike Aber-porth and Llangrannog, the village of Tresaith is of recent origin, for, until the mid-nineteenth century it consisted of two dwellings only – The Ship Inn and a thatched cottage. The Parry family who owned the Ship Inn were shipowners from about 1830 to 1905. Their first vessel the 'New Hope', a smack of 25 tons was actually built at Tresaith in 1827. The vessels operating from Tresaith – the 'Ruth', 'Margaret Ann' and the 'Lark' were small smacks bringing in coal, culm and limestone to the village. It was really during the last quarter of the nineteenth century that Tresaith grew into a village and contemporary newspaper reports referred to it as 'The Second Brighton'. It was really the popularity of the seaside holiday that brought it into being as a coastal settlement.

Throughout the Middle Ages, Aberystwyth was renowned

chiefly for its herring fisheries. Further developments were hampered however, by the repeated formation of a bar of stones and sand across the mouth of the harbour. This obstacle could only be cleared by the flooding of both rivers that temporarily scoured the channel. The presence of the bar handicapped all further development at Aberystwyth for many centuries. In 1561, it was described as ' . . . a barred haven of no valewe . . . ', and even by the mid-eighteenth century, the harbour had hardly improved at all.

Meanwhile, Aberdyfi to the north, though consisting of only a few houses, was recognised as the chief port along that part of the coast, and was the location of the Customs House. Around this time however, there came a significant impetus for the improvement of the harbour at Aberystwyth with the exploitation of the lead deposits of the Rheidol and Ystwyth valleys.

For a period of about forty years during the mid-nineteenth century, the port enjoyed a period of unprecedented commerical activity. The lead mines of northern Ceredigion were then at their busiest, and in 1851, of the 13,000 tons of goods exported from Aberystwyth, 10,500 tons were lead ore. The ore was loaded via a chute at the St David's Wharf and then shipped to the smelteries of Abertawe or Bristol. The imports were many and varied but timber, coal, slate, bricks and shop merchandise were the most important and reflected the growth of Aberystwyth as a genteel seaside resort in the mid-nineteenth century.

In 1864, the railway reached Aberystwyth, and after that the port entered a period of steady decline, with the harbour dues paid by vessels using the port reduced by more than half between 1860 and 1880. The decline was compounded by a fall in the demand for Welsh lead ore, caused by cheaper foreign imports, and the tonnage of ore exported from Aberystwyth fell from 2,385 tons in 1880 to 700 tons in 1890. Timber imports also fell as the shipbuilding industry declined. The port continued to deal in a considerable amount of general merchandise in the late nineteenth century but a trade in commodities such as soap, soda, candles and rice was hardly a substitute for the heavy tonnage of ore and timber dealt with earlier in the century.

Some six miles north of Aberystwyth and near the estuary of the Dyfi, lies the village of Borth, the most northerly port in Ceredigion. Although the main maritime activity of this area was concentrated in Aberdyfi across the river in Gwynedd, Borth itself also has a long maritime tradition. In the survey of 1566 it was described as:

'... the smale landinge place, Borthe ...'

and the estuary of the Dyfi was famed in the sixteenth and seventeenth centuries, for being the meeting place of all the area's herring boats at the commencement of the herring fishing season.

'... there is a wonderful great resorte of ffyshers assembled from all places ... and there is of the said companye there assembled, one chosen to be their admiral ...'

The Dyfi also provided the otherwise land-locked county of Montgomery, with its only maritime port – Cei Ward at Derwenlas, some five miles up the river from Aberdyfi.

The early village of Borth was located upon the higher ground at the southernmost end of the present settlement. Until the nineteenth century, the great marsh behind Borth, Cors Fochno, was completely undrained and the river Leri entered the sea at Aber-Leri, just north of the present village. It was at the mouth of the Leri that the *porth* – port – that gives the village its present name was located, and it was here until the mid-nineteenth century that both fishing sloops and trading smacks discharged their holds. All this changed, however, with the arrival of the Aberystwyth and Welsh coast railway in the area in 1863-64. The coastal trade of Borth was immediately hit, and after the departure of the sloop 'Prosperity' from Cei Ward late in 1863, the trade on the Dyfi to Derwenlas was also finished. Furthermore, in 1901, the course of the Leri was diverted to run directly into the Dyfi estuary as part of a scheme to drain Cors Fochno, thus eradicating all that remained of the former harbour at Borth. Thereafter, with the exception of the numerous families, such as the Bells who operated the ferry services from Ynyslas to Aberdyfi, the maritime activity of Borth ceased, and Ceredigion's northernmost port, like so many others in the county, has depended chiefly upon tourism ever since.

9
ABERYSTWYTH

Aberystwyth, home of the National Library of Wales and the oldest college of the University of Wales, is Ceredigion's largest and most important town. Following Llywelyn ap Gruffudd's resistance to Edward I campaign in 1277, a fortified castle was built on a hillock near the joint estuaries of the Rheidol and Ystwyth. The knoll, surrounded on the west side by marshes and on the south by the sea, was the ideal location for a defensive encampment. In addition, a shingle spur, Y Ro Wen, – extended southward from the knoll and this meant there was ample deep water available immediately below the town to provide an anchorage for ships. The town that grew around the castle was known as Llanbadarn Gaerog and it was not until Tudor times that the town was called Aberystwyth; an inappropriate name since the town was located at the mouth of the river Rheidol.

From the building of the castle in the 13th century until the dawn of the 18th century, Aberystwyth was moribund both as a town and military establishment. The castle was partly demolished by the Cromwellian army; a number of the inhabitants of the town in the middle ages were concerned with herring fishing in Bae Ceredigion, but on the whole it was a place of little consequence. Developments were hampered by the repeated formation of a bar of sand and stones across the mouth of the harbour and this obstacle could only be cleared by the flooding of the Ystwyth and Rheidol that temporarily scoured the channel. The presence of that bar handicapped all further development of the port and town of Aberystwyth. In 1561 it was described as 'a barred haven of no value' and even by the mid-eighteenth century the harbour had not been improved. Meanwhile, Aberdyfi to the north, although consisting of only a few cottages was recognised as the chief port of the region and was the location of the Customs House that controlled an extensive stretch of coast. In 1763 however, the removal of the Customs House to Aberystwyth indicated that there was development afoot. Then came a significant impetus for the improvement of the harbour at Aberystwyth via the tremendous exploitation of the lead and silver deposits of the Rheidol and Ystwyth valleys. It was realised that Aberystwyth was the most convenient port for the shipment of ores and from the 1780's onwards a number of attempts were made to improve the harbour. Some improvements were urgently needed since the trade of Aberystwyth was expanding rapidly with imports of wines, spirits, bricks, slate and coal complementing the growing exports of lead ore, pickled herrings and oak bark for the tanning industry. The growth in trade was also reflected in the growth of shipping. Whereas in 1701 only one small smack was registered at Aberystwyth, by 1799 there was 99 vessels registered there with a total tonnage of 3337.

The bar however, still remained the chief obstacle to the development of Aberystwyth as a port. The many schemes proposed for its eradication around the turn of the 18th century were only short term both in effect and scope. It was not until the 1830s when a comprehensive scheme involving the construction of a stone pier, in conjunction with the diversion of the rivers to scour the harbour mouth that the problem was really solved. Thereafter it was possible for larger vessels to enter the harbour without fear of being stranded there for many weeks. From the 1830s onwards, considerable quantities of timber for the shipbuilding industry that developed around the harbour was imported from the Baltic, Scandinavia and Canada. With regular passenger and goods sailing to Liverpool, Bristol and Ireland from around 1842 to the late 1860s, Aberystwyth developed into one of the most important ports on the coast of Bae Ceredigion. For a period of about forty years in the mid-nineteenth century, the port enjoyed a period unprecedented commercial activity. Between 1830 and 1870, 123 vessels ranging in size from small smacks to ocean-going barques were built at Aberystwyth by a number of family concerns. Shipbuilding in turn encouraged the development of a host of ancillary crafts such as block making, rope winding, sail making and iron founding.

The lead mines of northern Ceredigion were at their busiest and in the 1850s. Aberystwyth ships, together with vessels from other ports were heavily engaged in transporting ore to the smelteries of

Abertawe, Bristol and elsewhere. Down at the harbour-site prosperity was in the air but not all of that prosperity was based on commercial and industrial maritime activity. Aberystwyth was developing as a resort and for the gentry of mid-Wales and the border country, Aberystwyth became a genteel watering place. By 1810 the Marine Baths had appeared and by 1820, elegant Assembly Rooms had been built. Regency styled houses were also built and Aberystwyth developed as a town catering for the needs of the lesser gentry and the prosperous yeomen farmers from a wide area.

But in 1864 things were to change, for in that year the railway reached Aberystwyth and its arrival heralded a period of change and a different type of growth from earlier years. Hand in hand with the development of the railway, Aberystwyth was to develop phenomenally as a seaside resort; not as the somewhat staid watering resort for the aristocracy as in the mid-19th century but as a rather brash resort for the industrial workers of southern Wales and the Midlands who were accommodated in dozens of new boarding houses and hotels.

One of the hotels started during the 1860s was never finished but in 1867 it was purchased to become the main building of the new University of Wales. With the development of that college many of the residential facilities for tourists were taken over by the University or as accommodation for administrative buildings and student hostels. Aberystwyth developed as a centre of administration for an extensive region and its role as a summer holiday resort declined. This was especially true after 1950 as the University College expanded and as Aberystwyth's role as an administrative centre grew. Even its most elegant hotels were converted into offices for the local authority or into student hostels. The port of Aberystwyth too was declining. The opening of the narrow-gauge Vale of Rheidol railway in 1902 was seen by many as a means whereby the ore traffic might be revived, but the revival was short-lived and by the eve of the First World War, many of the northen Ceredigion mines had been abandoned and tourist traffic was rapidly becoming the mainstay of the Vale of Rheidol line. After 1918 there were few exports of lead ore from Aberystwyth, though small steam and motor coasters still brought the occasional cargo of timber to the port. Much of the facing stone for the National Library of Wales which was opened in 1937 arrived by sea and from the 1920s onwards roadstone from northern Wales was imported to the port by the old Cardiganshire County Council. Between 1920 and 1938, there was only 129 visits by trading vessels to Aberystwyth and this trade ceased completely during the Second World War.

Aberystwyth today is very much an administrative, cultural and educational centre, but it still possesses many features that one associates with a seaside holiday. These include the tall, multi-storeyed buildings that once accommodated extensive families for jolly boarding house holidays and the coastal railway that still grinds its way up the steep slopes of Constitution Hill and still runs its regular summer trips. On the top of that hill even the Camera Obscura, so beloved by the Victorian holiday maker, has been restored to provide a spectacular view over the town and bay. The band stand still has an occasional summer show but in the heyday of Victorian enterprise the jewel was certainly the pier, originally an 800 ft structure opened in 1864. On Good Friday of the year it was opened, no fewer that 7,800 people paid their tolls for the privilege of perambulating along it. In January 1865 a storm washed away 100 feet of pier although it was rebuilt a few years later. In 1938 half of it was taken away in a storm and bits of it have fallen into disrepair ever since with the result that what now remains is barely 300 feet long.

10
ABERAERON

Aberaeron is the nearest thing we have in Ceredigion to a planned town and its development during the first half of the 19th century is almost entirely due to the effort of the Rev. Alban Thomas Jones Gwynne of Tyglyn and his son of the same name who built the mansion Mynachdy in 1825. Tradition has it that the town was designed by the famous architect John Nash, who was a native of the town of Aberteifi. Although John Nash who was a family friend of the Gwynnes may have had a hand in the 'outline planning' of the town, most of the houses were built after his death and Edward Haycock, a well-known Shrewsbury architect has been suggested as the prime planner of the Georgian town.

Aberaeron, until the building of the harbour between 1807 and 1811, was merely a landing creek at the mouth of the river Aeron. The bar at the mouth of the river was a considerable hazard to navigation and the amount of shingle deposited on the beach meant that vessels could be landlocked for considerable periods. The nearest village of Llanddewi Aberarth with its shipbuilding yard, its fishing weirs and harbour facilities was a far more important settlement than Aberaeron. Through the efforts of Rev. Gwynne however, all that was to change and in 1807 work commenced on building two piers to protect a safe harbour. 'These improvements were done at the expense of the Reverend Alban Thomas Jones Gwynne, Lord of the Manor' said the *Cambrian Journal* in 1811 'who spared no expense to rendering the work as complete as possible and who said also to give liberal encouragement to the person as may be disposed to take building leases near the harbour'. Gradually a planned town was erected around the harbour and Alban Square, named after the founder, was a gem of Georgian planning. With the construction of the harbour, maritime trade at Aberaeron increased considerably at the expense of Llanddewi Aberarth. By 1830, John Harries and Evan Jones (from Aberarth) were in business as substantial shipbuilders in Aberaeron and by 1850 twenty three men were employed in the industry. The harbour had its regular sea service to Bristol and to

Liverpool and most of the essentials required by the people of the Aeron valley were imported through the busy port, until the death knell was sounded by the arrival of the railway from Llanbedr Pont Steffan in 1911.

Not only was Aberaeron an important port in the 19th century, it was also developing as a very desirable seaside resort and its Chalybeate well became a considerable attraction in an age when 'taking the waters' was regarded as a cure for many illnesses. A variety of craft enterprises developed on the banks of the Aeron which include a substantial woollen mill that operated between 1820 and 1950. Here, too, in a riverside forge the long-handled Aberaeron shovel that was used in many parts of Wales and Ireland was pressed by generations of remarkable blacksmiths from the establishment of the business in 1850.

11
CEINEWYDD *(NEW QUAY)*

It may be a misnomer to describe Ceinewydd as a town, despite the fact that it has its own Town Council and Mayor, but it is the best example, not only in Ceredigion but arguably in the whole of Wales of a community where life was completely tied up with the sea. It was really 'the Clydeside' of 19th century western Wales for the shipbuilding industry was of considerable importance in its development and more than 200 ships, some ocean going were built there and on the adjacent beaches of Traethgwyn and Cei-bach.

The sheltered harbour did not really develop as a shipbuilding and trading centre until the early nineteenth century. Like many other coastal settlements in Bae Ceredigion, Ceinewydd before the early nineteenth century boom in shipbuilding and maritime trade, consisted of only a few thatched cottages above the beach with agricultural land around them. Its natural harbour provided shelter for fishermen and the few trading vessels that entered the port but in the 1820s, in particular, trade was increasing very rapidly and improvements to the harbour become necessary. In 1835 the 'New Quay Harbour Act' was passed and a stone pier was built at a cost of £7,000. This brought great prosperity to the village and new houses were built on what had previously been agricultural land.

It was not as a trading port that Ceinewydd earned its reputation however, but as one of the most important shipbuilding ports in southern Wales. With the very rapid expansion in shipowning, a source of supply for the new vessels had to be found. Ceinewydd become one of the main suppliers of these vessels and many ships of varying sizes and types were built by a number of competent shipwrights. In reality there were three shipbuilding centres; Ceinewydd itself which developed rapidly as a maritime community with its houses rising in steep terraces from a wide sheltered harbour; Traethgwyn, a curving bay just to the north of Ceinewydd where in recent years erosion has removed many of the dwellings located there and Cei-bach, a long stony beach below wooded cliffs, sheltered from the winds by Llanina Point. At the height of the shipbuilding boom in the 1840s it has been estimated that over three hundred skilled workmen were employed in ship construction. The many shipbuilders of the area not only produced small smacks and schooners designed for sailing along the coast but were also concerned with building larger vessels that sailed to North and South America and as far as China and Australia. Ceinewydd not only had its shipwrights but also the ancillary trades essential in a shipbuilding centre. It had half a dozen blacksmiths shops, three sail making lofts, three rope walks and a foundry concerned with making windlasses and winches for the vessels built in the village and its environs.

Every section of the Ceinewydd community was tied with the sea. Most of its male inhabitants were mariners for although shipbuilding in the village had ceased by the 1870s many of the men of the village still went to sea, sailing from the great ports of Britain. The village still had its private schools where navigation was taught until the end of the nineteenth century and many of the last square riggers that sailed world-wide were captained by Ceinewydd men. The complete crew of a sailing vessel trading with South America and the Pacific coast of North America often came from the same village. The loss of a vessel, and a very large number were lost, would often place a whole village in mourning. Today, Ceinewydd is a busy holiday and yachting centre, and the many people who visit the village have no conception of the contribution that its mariners and shipbuilders made to the development of maritime trade in the nineteenth century.

It is now a hundred and fifty years since the last Ceinewydd built ship was launched, but in the tourist orientated settlement there are many pieces in existence that point to the importance of the sea in influencing the lives of its inhabitants. Disused warehouses, now cafes and places of entertainment, may still be seen near the water's edge. Lengths of chain and metal rings and capstans are still in place and the toll of charges for export and import may still be seen on the exterior wall near the harbourmaster's office. The names of ships long since gone are preserved in the names of houses, while many may still be

Edwards Warehouse, Mercantile Quay, Aberteifi, c.1880.

The crew of S.S. Italiana *owned by Aberporth business-men and manned by local sea-men, 1912.*

The S.S. Italiana.

The coaster Iris *passing Pwll y Castell to the port of Aberteifi* (Cardigan), *c.1930.*

Gwalia Garage, Aberteifi.

Hand-carved love spoons.

A quoits match at Horeb, Llandysul.

Seine netting on the river Dyfi, 1970.

The frame of a Teifi coracle.

Fred Llewelyn the coracle king, Cenarth.

Seine netsmen at Patch in the Teifi estuary.

A cottage hearth from north Pembrokeshire but similar to a large number found in Ceredigion.

A two roomed cottage central Ceredigion.

A one roomed cottage central Ceredigion.

A typical farmhouse kitchen.

Mrs Nan Jones, Cartrefle, Sarnau,
Ceredigion, using washing dolly.

Oatcake making, 1970.

Yr Hafod, Pontarfynach.

Trawscoed.

Plas Gogerddan.

Rhydcolomennod, Llangrannog.

Penparcau toll-gate, c.1910.

South-gate Toll house, from Penparcau, Aberystwyth
(now at the Museum of Welsh Life St. Ffagan).

A long-house with family and animals under the same roof.

Aberaeron.

Aberporth, the ship beach – Traeth y Llongau.

Aberporth, c.1890.

5 pleasure boats operating off beach, Aberystwyth in 1930s.

Aberystwyth beach, c.1938.

Cardigan Harbour 1812.

The square at Llanddewi Brefi, c.1930.

Llangrannog, c.1890.

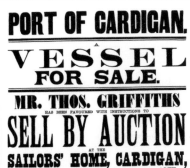

PORT OF CARDIGAN.

VESSEL
FOR SALE.

MR. THOS. GRIFFITHS

HAS BEEN FAVOURED WITH INSTRUCTIONS TO

SELL BY AUCTION

AT THE

SAILORS' HOME, CARDIGAN,

On Saturday, the 13th of January, 1877,

THAT WELL-BUILT AND FAST-SAILING SMACK, CALLED

"CHARMING NANCY,"

(REGISTER TONNAGE, 21 TONS)

WILL CARRY FROM 36 TO 38 TONS; DRAUGHT OF WATER, 7½ FEET.

This Smack is in very good order, having undergone a thorough repair about
five years ago, and is now READY for SEA, and may be inspected at the
NETPOOL, CARDIGAN.

For further particulars apply to Capt. DAVID EVANS, Owr, Saint Dogmells

CREDIT ON CONDITIONS.—SALE TO COMMENCE AT 2 O'CLOCK.

Cardigan, December 15th, 1876.

J. C. ROBERTS, PRINTER, &c., "OBSERVER" OFFICE, 1, EBEN'S LANE, CARDIGAN.

PORT OF CARDIGAN.

FISHING SMACK FOR SALE.

MR.R.M.ROBERTS

HAS RECEIVED INSTRUCTIONS TO SELL BY

AUCTION

AT THE

MARINERS' ARMS, ST. DOGMELLS,

At 5 o'clock in the Afternoon,

On Saturday, the 7th day of September, 1878,

THAT WELL-KNOWN AND FAST-SAILING

FISHING SMACK

CALLED

THE "ARROW"

OF CARDIGAN,

In first-class condition, with new TRAWLING GEAR, and now lying on the
Beach at ST. DOGMELLS, near Cardigan, where it may be inspected. The "Arrow"
is well known as a fast, safe, and seaworthy Boat, and highly adapted for the
Herring Fisheries.

For further particulars apply to Mr. Thomas Evans, Shipbuilder, St. Dogmells

J. C. ROBERTS, PRINTER, "OBSERVER" OFFICE, 1, EBEN'S LANE, CARDIGAN.

To be Sold by Auction,

ON MONDAY, THE 20th DAY OF MAY, 1844.

BY MR. D. ROBERTS,

At the Angel Hotel, Cardigan,

At Three o' Clock in the Afternoon.

ALL THAT FAST-SAILING

Smack,

CALLED

THE MARIA,

WITH ALL HER MATERIALS.

Will carry 58 Tons;

Tresaith 1880s.

crammed with souvenirs from abroad; paintings of Vesuvius in full eruption, delicate tea sets from Japan and paintings of graceful sailing vessels entering harbour or fighting the angry seas.

12
RURAL INDUSTRIES

Ceredigion is an area of cultural and scenic variety and as far as rural industry is concerned there are differences between the various districts of the county. For instance, the industrial activity that characterised the coastal towns and villages was quite different from that which characterised the upland core of the county and also different from the rural craft activity which dominated the valleys of the main rivers that flowed into Bae Ceredigion.

In upland Ceredigion and its self sufficing economy, there were always one or two people although not trained as craftsmen who were more competent than others in producing the necessities of life. Perhaps one smallholder would earn a local reputation as a carver of shepherd's crooks or hand rakes and another would have a reputation for making horse-drawn sledges or lip-work seed baskets and neighbours would go to them for the supply of those essentials. These were the part-time, amateur craftsmen with dextrous hands (y dynion dethe) who were an important element in most rural communities.

Ceredigion with its long coastline and villages that seem to cling to the edge of a land witnessed a craft activity that was completely different from that of the agricultural sections of the county. Here were the highly specialised craftsmen who fulfilled the needs of those whose livelihood depended on the sea and its harvest. Boat builders and rope makers, copper workers, anchor smiths, sail makers, net makers and pulley block makers were all of considerable importance in the sea-orientated villages and towns of Ceredigion. Following the demise of coastal trading activity and the spectacular decline in in-shore fishing, most of those skills have long disappeared.

Of course, throughout the centuries the market towns of Ceredigion supported a large number of craftsmen who supplied the needs of a town's hinterland who regarded Aberteifi or Llanbedr Pont Steffan or Aberystwyth as their own market town. Some indication of the importance of the country towns as suppliers of goods is provided by the following examples from early nineteenth century 'Trade Directories':

Aberteifi in 1830 had:

3 Bakers
13 Boot makers
2 Coopers
5 Dressmakers and Milliners
2 Straw-Hat makers
2 Weavers
4 Blacksmiths
3 Curriers
3 Saddlers
6 Tailors
2 Whitesmiths (Tinsmiths)
1 Corn miller
7 Carpenters
4 Glaziers
5 Maltsers
2 Printers
2 Tanners
1 Stone mason

In addition, as an important port it also supported an anchor smith, 2 shipbuilders, 2 pulley block makers and 3 sail makers together with a number of foundry workers employed in one of the two foundries that were concerned with producing agricultural as well as maritime essentials.

Aberaeron in the same year, although not yet fully developed as a port, had:

1 Woollen manufacturer
1 Boot maker
1 Baker
1 Carpenter
1 Corn miller
1 Hat maker
1 Blacksmith
2 Shipwrights

1 Blacksmith and Shovel Maker

Aberystwyth in 1830 had:

8 Bakers	2 Tin smiths
11 Carpenters & Joiners	2 Hat makers
2 Dress makers	4 Tanners
7 Tailors	1 Cooper
20 Boot makers	5 Cabinet makers
3 Curriers	8 Stone masons
6 Maltsters	2 Corn millers
4 Saddlers	2 Skinners
2 Straw-hat makers	3 Wheelwrights
1 Brewer	1 Nail maker
4 Lime burners	1 Rope maker
3 Shipwrights	1 Sail maker

Of course it was not only the market towns of Ceredigion that supplied the day to day requirements of the population since every village and rural neighbourhood had its own contingent of craftsmen who supplied essentials. They also made tools and utensils and the whole range of goods that the community required. In the production of hand tools for agriculture, and much of the craft activity in Ceredigion was connected with this work, each craftsman was concerned with producing equipment suited to the needs of a locality. Local conditions of topography, soil and vegetation were all factors that affected the design of tools. For example, the Aberaeron billhook, whose design was limited to Ceredigion was a tool specifically designed to deal with the heavy thorn growth of Ceredigion hedges. The long-handled triangular-bladed Aberaeron shovel was designed for use on steep slopes while horse-drawn ploughs built at such places as Llanfihangel-y-Creuddyn, Sarnau, Ffostrasol and Betws were well suited to deal with the soil of the locality in which they were used.

One example will suffice to illustrate the importance of the craftsman in village life. The small south Ceredigion village of Rhydlewis in 1890 had:

2 Carpenters	1 Tanner	6 Bootmakers
1 Stone mason	2 Corn millers	1 Blacksmith
1 Leather currier	3 Clog makers	8 Weavers
1 Baker	1 Basket maker	2 Saddlers
5 Tailors	1 Pin maker	

It is clear, therefore, that a rural county like Ceredigion had a great variety of industry and it is only during the present century that the age-old pattern of life, where the craftsman was an important element of the population, has been eroded.

The craft industries of Ceredigion may be divided into the following broad categories:

1. *Extractive Industries* such as lead and silver extraction employed specialised craftsmen within the industry. Blacksmiths, woodworkers, pattern makers and brass founders were all essential for the smooth running of an extractive venture and many of the mines of northern Ceredigion were self-sufficient in equipment and structures. In this category too, are the self sufficing activities of peat cutting, especially important in the hill districts and on the low-lying marshes of Cors Fochno and Cors Caron. There were also in Ceredigion a short-lived ventures like the extraction of sea salt at Ynyslas.

2. *Processing Industries* where raw materials produced within the area were converted for use by the people or for working on by another craftsman. Thus, the many tanneries of the county produced leather that could be made into a finished product by saddlers and bootmakers. Of the processing crafts, the most important were corn milling, tanning, woollen manufacturing, limestone burning and barley malting. Most of these trades had to be carried out in purpose-built or converted buildings and most required a wide range of static equipment. In most cases water-power was required to operate machinery and consequently most of the industries occupied valley locations.

3. *Creative Crafts* were usually carried out by individual craftsmen in workshops. In some cases, such as in tailoring, saddlery and dress-making where the tools of operation were few and light, itinerant craftsmen who were able to visit the remotest of farmsteads were once commonplace in Ceredigion. Creative crafts fall into three distinct groups:

a) *Those concerned with supplying the day to day needs of a local community.* These were the crafts essential to every self sufficing group and included blacksmithing, carpentry, undertaking, stone masonry, tailoring, book making and basket making. Some of the maritime trades of the past were also in this category.

b) *Crafts that came into existence because of the presence of a particular raw material.* These included bowl turning, wood carving and tool handle making, all of which utilized the heavy timber of the Teifi valley. There was also the production of clog soles for the clog making factories of the north of England by itinerant woodworkers who used the alder trees of the county. Hat making, especially in the Tre'r-ddol, and Penuwch districts where there were ample supplies of wool, was another craft.

c) *Home Crafts* such as butter and cheese making, bread making, beer brewing and amateur activities such as embroidery and needlework, straw-lip work and spoon carving, were often carried out as spare-time leisure activities.

One of the most widespread of all the rural industries of Ceredigion was that of corn milling and a water-driven mill could be seen on the bank of most streams. In the nineteen twenties, there was as many as 82 operating in Ceredigion. The Teifi valley, was a centre of the wool textile industry. That industry was to develop spectacularly in the 19th century to meet the ever growing demand for flannel shirts and underwear for the industrial workers of southern Wales. The Teifi valley supplied that industrial market while in the north of the county woollen mills in such places as Tal-y-bont were largely concerned with supplying the requirements of the lead miners of the region. Other mills in the county were very much concerned with meeting the local demand. The textile worker was as essential to the rural population as the blacksmith or carpenter, supplying flannel, knitting wool, blankets and tweed for largely self-sufficient rural communities.

13
CHURCH AND CHAPEL

When one looks at the Ceredigion of today, one remarkable feature is the large number of places of worship that seem to dominate the landscape. Tiny villages may have two or three chapels and churches, each one representing some aspect of Christian doctrine that is no longer relevant, except to scholars of theology. In uninhabited valleys and on empty hillsides, chapel buildings that can seat substantial congregations in some discomfort still exist and although many closed their doors years ago, others still attract minuscule congregations on the Sabbath. Calvinistic Methodists and Anglicans, Roman Catholics and Unitarians, Congregationalists and Baptists and other shades of belief are well represented and a visitor to Ceredigion could be forgiven for thinking that he was in a land where the population was caught up in a fervour of Christian worship. But many of those chapels and churches closed years ago and others have been converted into carpet warehouses, garages and tourist amenities. Religious affiliation and church going is no longer the dominant force of communal life.

Nevertheless, since church and chapel-going was such a force in moulding the life of many generations of Cardis, the relevance of ecclesiastical buildings cannot be ignored. After all, Ceredigion's many churches were founded by itinerant Celtic missionaries in the Dark Ages and its population for centuries was devoutly Catholic. Ceredigion was also the power-house of the Methodist Revival of the 18th century. Here, too, the explosive force of the revivals of 1859 and 1904 swept through the county like a hurricane leaving a deep impression on the life and behaviour of its inhabitants long after the fervour of revival was a spent force.

In the 5th and 6th century A.D. Britain in common with the other countries of western Europe witnessed a rapid expansion in Christian teaching. In the expansion of Christianity, Wales received its teaching from the travelling missionaries of the Celtic Church. Many of those utilised the well-travelled trade routes of Atlantic Europe, travelling by sea to establish a large number of religious settlements not only in Wales but also in Ireland, Cornwall and Brittany. To these early saints who brought the ascetic austerity of the early Celtic Church to Wales, the sea constituted a main road rather than an obstacle. Many of the religions communities they set up in Ceredigion were in fairly close proximity to the sea and near sandy beaches where frail vessels could be safely landed. In addition, as in later centuries, Ceredigion had links across the Irish Sea with Gaelic Christianity and saints like St Breda *(Ffraid)* established settlements in Kildare as well as in Ceredigion, as did St Caron. From northern Wales came Tysilio and Deiniol, while St Padarn came from south-eastern Wales when the Celtic Church was well established. All in all, Ceredigion in the Dark Ages had a large number of *Llannau* (sing. *Llan*) dedicated to missionaries who brought the Christian faith to Ceredigion.

Undoubtedly, for centuries the Celtic Church in Ceredigion existed and flourished as an independent body but with the arrival of the Norman conquerors all that was to change and the church had to conform to the rigours of Roman Catholicism and lose its independence. In the Celtic Church, ecclesiastical communities were cared for by groups of clerics who lived together in a small group. The Normans demolished known religious communities and the land and endowments they held were transferred to rich French or English monasteries. At Llanbadarn, for instance, monks from Gloucester established a priory. Although another Priory was established in Aberteifi, the most spectacular, influential and rich ecclesiastical settlement was Ystrad Fflur *(Strata Florida)* abbey. Established by the Cistercian order in 1164 the great monastery that took three years in its construction was built of stone from the Bristol area, brought by sea to the port of Llanddewi Aberarth and then overland to the remote corner of what was to become Ceredigion. For those one and a half centuries, until the dissolution of the monasteries by Henry VIII in 1539, Ystrad Fflur flourished and the order owned substantial acreage of land in mid and north Ceredigion. The monks farmed the land themselves: they encouraged the development of wool production and the textile industry; they had many tenants who owed them allegiance and service and Ystrad Fflur was a considerable influence in the economic development and in the social and cultural life of the area. Undoubtedly, Roman Catholicism took a firm root in medieval Ceredigion, for the faith with its rigid beliefs and organised system suited a rural population who themselves lived a rigidly organised life. Above all, Catholicism provided a priesthood that was of the people; priests whose background was similar to that of their congregations. It was Roman Catholicism that encouraged the flowering of the Welsh cultural life that expressed itself in poetry and in the transcription of printed manuscripts; the Church was a patron of the arts and it brought security within insecurity which was all the people demanaded of it.

In Wales generally, the Reformation was largely a matter of English politics that failed to arouse any fervour and enthusiasm amongst the native population. During the earlier years of the Reformation, the religious changes were overshadowed by the Act of Union with England. Isolated by his ignorance of the English language, deserted by the aristocracy who had become anglicised under the Tudors, life for the Cardi deteriorated greatly. To him, the Reformation meant theft of land and the destruction of monasteries and abbeys. The bulk of the population understood little of the new faith preached to them in an alien tongue by priests who were not of their own. Tithes had to be paid and although, outwardly the people may have been forced to turn to Anglicanism, they still clung tenaciously to their old beliefs and traditions. In some parishes, services were infrequent and in many cases a parish priest was responsible for many churches. For example, the vicar of Llannerch Aeron in 1750 had to look after other parish churches at Llannarth, Llanina, Llanddewi Aberarth, Ciliau Aeron, Llansanffraid, Llanrhystud, Llanbadarn Trefeglwys and even Llanfihangel-y-Creuddyn thirty miles away. Ceredigion was in a deep religious torpor served by an anglicised and underpaid priesthood.

The Puritan movement of the 17th century also failed to arouse the fervour and enthusiasm of Ceredigion as a whole. Its earnest, well meaning travelling preachers, preached deeply philosophical sermons and frowned upon all enjoyment. Nevertheless, a number of nonconformist Independent and Baptist causes were established in southern Ceredigion. Many of them, in the early days, met surreptitiously in barns and remote farmsteads but in 1689 they were allowed by law to establish places of worship. Congregations were very small, for this was a religion for those of independent mind; it appealed to reason rather than the heart and as such did not really appeal to a large proportion of the population of Ceredigion. All the ingredients were here for a sudden intellectual and moral expansion and that came in the form of a religious revival great in its intensity and consequences. The armament of Welsh Methodism was the explosive force of enthusiasm, and one of its leaders said 'we preach to the heart so that there be faith in the heart rather than enlightenment in the head'. Methodism attempted to bridle fervour and harness enthusiasm to the service of personal salvation. Its armament was not the reasoned prose of the earlier Puritans but the oratorical *hwyl* of revival and the hymns of William Williams. Above all, it was a movement that had its origin in the very heart of Wales and in Ceredigion, the remote village of Llangeitho was the fountain head for a revival that swept the Welsh countryside like a storm. Undoubtedly, it was Calvinistic Methodism that became the most important and widespread of all religious affiliations and Calvinism with its other-worldly aspirations and feelings of personal salvation had a profound effect on the life and morality of the people of Ceredigion. The stranglehold of Nonconformity became even greater with the earnest revivals of 1859 and 1904 that swept the country.

Unlike Calvinistic Methodism which had its roots in upland Wales, Wesleyan Methodism was an import brought into the north of the county by immigrants from Cornwall who came to work in the prosperous lead mines of the hill country in northern Ceredigion. Here, in villages such as Ystumtuen and Goginan, Wesleyan churches flourished. In the Teifi valley, which saw prosperity as a centre of the wool textile industry, another import, Unitarianism, became a force in the religious life of the 18th and 19th century. This denomination with its reasoned arguments appealed to practical people concerned with making a living in a highly competitive industry and as such its beliefs appealed to the practical and independent of mind. In its denial of the Holy Trinity, Unitarianism drew the wrath of the orthodox denominations and the area where Unitarianism held sway became known as the Black Spot – *Y Smotyn Du*.

14
EPILOGUE

The pattern of life when the inhabitants of Ceredigion looked no further than the boundaries of their own neighbourhood or an adjacent market town for all their necessities has changed very greatly in the twentieth century. The 1914-1918 war was certainly a watershed between the ancient, unchanging way of life and the demise of the rural neighbourhood as an economic and social entity. After the second world war that change was completed as the natural resources of the country side were less effectively exploited. The products of modern, international industry became increasingly available, even in the remotest corners of the county. The raw materials, once regarded as essential for the survival of a community, became neglected and the once vital skills of the countryman have long been forgotten. Mass production, mass transportation and mass advertising all played their part in the break-up of the ageless pattern of life and in the obliteration of many a rural skill.

Of course, in the Ceredigion of the 21st century, craft work of all kinds has become the flagship of a flourishing and ever developing tourist industry and the hand craftsman has become the cornerstone of many facilities concerned with the interpretation of the more recent traditions of the people of Wales. Whether more than a handful of those artisans represent the authentic traditions of the country is very questionable indeed. Many of the products that emanate from the workshops of Ceredigion today have precious little to do with the traditional craftsmanship of the countryside where utilitarian needs were inevitably married to beauty of form and good design. Only a few of the age-old crafts of Ceredigion have survived into the late twentieth century for the majority of craftsmen today produce goods that appeal very largely to a tourist market.

Nevertheless, a few skilled men have been able to meet the challenge of changing demands. One or two blacksmiths, for example, produce wrought iron work of supreme quality and others have taken advantage of the vogue for horse-riding to act as farriers, but in general, the traditional craftsmanship of Ceredigion has changed beyond recognition. Local raw materials are hardly ever used today and skills that were once commonplace in the countryside have disappeared completely from contemporary workshops. Yet, the revival of forgotten skills could have some relevance in the future in a post-industrial era when oil resources begin to run dry or in the face of a catastrophic collapse of our economic system. Then the skills of the past may at least, provide a basis for survival.